POETICALLY ME
BY
VICTORIA AMIDOU

POETICALLY ME

Victoria Amidou

P.O. Box 085137

Racine, Wisconsin 53408

www.victoriaamidou.com

This book or parts thereof may not be reproduced in any form, stored in a retrieval system or transmitted in any form by any means; electronic, mechanical, photocopy, recording or otherwise without written permission of the publisher, except as provided by United States of America copyright law.

Copyright © 2016 by Victoria Amidou

Published 2016

Published in the United States of America 2016 by Victoria Amidou

ISBN-13: 978-0692642016

ISBN-10: 0692642013

ACKNOWLEDGEMENTS

It is my esteemed pleasure to again thank God for allowing me to be his vessel. I in no way would be able to write the way in which I do if it were not for the anointing that God has placed on my life.

Also by Victoria Amidou

El Shaddai -My One True Love - Print and EBook

For True - Spoken Word Album – Cd and Digital

TABLE OF CONTENTS

COPYRIGHT

ACKNOWLEDGEMENTS

TABLE OF CONTENTS

INTRODUCTION

« CHAPTER 1 »

« CHAPTER 2 »

« CHAPTER 3 »

« CHAPTER 4 »

« CHAPTER 5 »

« CHAPTER 6 »

« CHAPTER 7 »

« CHAPTER 8 »

« CHAPTER 9 »

« CHAPTER 10 »

« CHAPTER 11 »

« CHAPTER 12 »

« CHAPTER 13 »

« CHAPTER 14 »

« CHAPTER 15 »

« CHAPTER 16 »

« CHAPTER 17 »

« CHAPTER 18 »

« CHAPTER 19 »

« CHAPTER 20 »

« CHAPTER 21 »

« CHAPTER 22 »

« CHAPTER 23 »

« CHAPTER 24 »

« CHAPTER 25 »

« CHAPTER 26 »

« CHAPTER 27 »

« CHAPTER 28 »

« CHAPTER 29 »

« CHAPTER 30 »

« CHAPTER 31 »

« CHAPTER 32 »

« CHAPTER 33 »

« CHAPTER 34 »

« CHAPTER 35 »

« CHAPTER 36 »

« CHAPTER 37 »

« CHAPTER 38 »

« CHAPTER 39 »

« CHAPTER 40 »

« CHAPTER 41 »

« CHAPTER 42 »

« CHAPTER 43 »

« CHAPTER 44 »

« CHAPTER 45 »

« CHAPTER 46 »

« CHAPTER 47 »

« CHAPTER 48 »

« CHAPTER 49 »

« CHAPTER 50 »

« CHAPTER 51 »

« CHAPTER 52 »

« CHAPTER 53 »

« CHAPTER 54 »

« CHAPTER 55 »

« CHAPTER 56 »

« CHAPTER 57 »

« CHAPTER 58 »

« CHAPTER 59 »

« CHAPTER 60 »

« CHAPTER 61 »

APPENDIX

NOTES

AUTHOR LINKS

OVERVIEW

There is nothing more rewarding than truly loving yourself, for it is through loving yourself that you are better able to love other's.

Victoria Amidou

INTRODUCTION

There is a great honor that comes with being able to put my pen to the pad and write for relief. My ability to do so has taken me on a journey that I would not have otherwise been able to take.

As I have navigated my way through each and every one of these poems that God has so graciously allowed me to write I am taken back to the very moments that each and every one of them were birthed into this realm.

I will forever be in awe of the sheer awesomeness of my gift from God and I will never take for granted that which he has blessed me with.

A writer is more so who I am and not just what I do. Writing is etched in my SPIRIT and fused to my DNA.

« CHAPTER 1 »

A Cry from Within

As I sit here and wonder who I am and who I could have been.

My heart bleeds as tears fall from within.

Whose child am I?

What's my purpose for being?

Is it to cry?

Is it to constantly wonder why?

Is it to remain totally paralyzed from the fear that I feel when people try to get near?

I shatter at the thought of never knowing who I could have been, so much so that I cry tears of blood from within.

My heart aches from this agonizing pain that I feel.

I wish this was a dream, oh God I wish this wasn't real.

As I gaze into the mirror at my face on a daily base's I soon start to see visions of it being erased.

My face and my pain seems to be one and the same.

I need someone to need me.

I want someone to want me.

I have desires for me soul to be debt free.

Continuously I wonder why I see so much pain in my eyes.

Is it because I feel my own demise?

A Cry from Within was written from a place of pain. When I read this back to myself after writing it I wondered, is there someone else out there who feels like this?

I was at a pivotal point in my life where my pain was screaming to be set free. I walked around constantly crying inside because I felt as though I had yet again failed myself. I had not learned to give God my pain.

« CHAPTER 2 »

A Greater Love Than This

A mother carrying her child.

Feel my heart beat, wow!

Thump, thump, beat, beat.

Hear my fears running, oh, so deep.

Can I carry you to term?

Or will my prayers go unheard?

Thump, thump, beat, beat.

As I feel your moments in my womb, my heart aches from this inevitable doom.

A Greater Love than this I will someday have replace this feeling of gloom.

Born to soon, how could this be?

Will my heart mend and my mind replace this agonizing memory?

Thump, thump, beat, beat.

A Greater Love than this will you please give me.

Wanting, wishing, hoping to be free.

How can this pain ever release me?

Failing to overstand while consumed by my fears.

How, oh how, will my soul ever be clear?

Trapped by my pain, while trying to maintain.

Struggling to get by while tears fall from my eyes.

Thump, thump, beat, beat.

God please set my soul debt free and grant me a Greater Love than this to replace what was taken from me.

A Greater Love Than This was written during a time when my family suffered great loss. Death is a very painful thing for the love ones who are left behind to carry the burden of coping with the loss. But when you are a mother and your child is still in your womb and the death occurs, it leaves a gaping hole in the very fiber of your being.

You mourn the loss in a way in which no one else can identify. The pain never goes away. All you can do is pray for God to be your strength and to love you pass your pain.

« CHAPTER 3 »

A Minister's Wife

To step outside your normal boundaries and accept one of the biggest challenges that life has to offer become a minister's wife.

Being a minister's wife has many advantages such as being able to pray for those who are in need.

Holding onto life with grace and spiritual clarity.

Picking up the pieces of life when there too small for the normal eyes to see.

Grabbing a hold of life with un-denying curiosity.

Being able to leap over life's problems without a single frown.

Holding your partners hand and reassure him that God knows his plan.

Being a minister's wife takes a great amount of courage and a greater amount of faith.

For after long days and bountiful praise a minister needs his wife loving gaze.

A minister's wife is on her knees with her man praying to God for healing of their land, more unity in their nation, a more spiritual congregation.

She may not be covered from head to toe.

She may not have children that are all grown up, you know.

She may not be all glitzes and glamour.

She may just be handy with a garden tool or even a hammer.

She may just be the sweet lady with a beautiful smile.

She may just be the one that makes you laugh out loud.

When you think of a minister's wife, you should think of diligence, determination, devotion, diplomacy, and death.

Death to the old and birth to the new.

For new horizons are her area to conquer.

A minister's wife is in a class all by herself.

She thinks of God always before anyone else.

She puts God above all else.

She is mesmerized by her will to do his work at best.

She is striving always to be a step above the rest.

Not to boast or brag about the deeds she's done but to please the Lord for whom is heaven adorned.

She's not prideful nor is she a people pleaser.
She's a minister's wife, God's deed squeezer.
Squeezing out hope when no one else has none.
Searching the skies for Heaven's Holy Son.
Smiling with faith when all else fails.
Crying happy tears when God prevails.
She's a minister's wife sent here by God to climb all unspiritual hills by doing his work at will.

A Minister's Wife is one of my favorite poems. It is acknowledging the women who serve alongside God's spokesmen. That duty is a very demanding one for all the women involved because they are required to move even when their bodies don't want too.

When life is on overload and no one seems to care that they are indeed to human. I can identify with that because I am a mother to many children. I admire the women who have this duty because serving God for yourself is a full time job and they have chosen to reach out to an entire congregation.

May God continue to bless all of you who have made the choice to do this faithfully.

« CHAPTER 4 »

Ageless

Caress me with your strong arms.

Turn me on with your magnetic charm.

Gaze into my beautiful eyes and fill my heart with sweet lies.

Lay my soft body down and work your magical hands.

Those of which should be heaven bound.

Touch me, taunt me, tease me, but baby never stop without pleasing me.

Sensual from my head to my toes.

But most importantly my ears are aching for your voice to say hello.

Your smile, your frown, even the way you lay my body down, are all the things that make you true.

Time is the essence of this occasion.

Our bodies joined in this bitter sweet revelation.

Ageless is what I am in spite of whatever should become of our union tonight, as we bask in this intense creation of human procreation.

Ageless was written when I was of course at another pivotal point in my life and thinking of being blessed to live to see another year.

In some instances, in life age has no boundaries when it comes to a mother loving her child, a husband loving his wife, or God loving us.

Love is a very powerful thing that surpasses even time. When you are in love with someone you are taken in by the sheer blessing of it all. You want everything to be right and you are very eager to please.

You forget that you're no longer twenty-one and your get up and go, has got up and went. That those long brisk walks have turned into short slow trots and that beautiful sandy hair has begun to turn gray, but all that is okay because true love can see pass those days.

« CHAPTER 5 »

All Wide Up

All wide up, what you say?

Trying so hard to get away.

From my broken dreams.

Misplaced trust and dreadful things.

All wide up, open to the world.

Wondering why I was never daddy's little girl?

Trying to refrain from being insane, hoping and praying to just hold on and maintain.

All wide up, here I go again!

Crushed by broken promises.

Lost by illicit dreams.

Trying to figure out why is all this attacking me?

All wide up and I don't know what to do until I hear a voice and it happens to be you.

My Dear Savior telling me to hold on until he goes to the mighty man who lives upstairs to clear a trail ending all my despair.

Then I smiled and felt a great relief because I knew that man was going to save me in his son's Jesus name as long as I repent and maintain. All wide up, now on a good thang!

All wide up is about being under the influence of God so much so that it takes over your very being. I love when I am operating in God's Divine presence. I hear him, I feel him, and I know that he knows me because through all that I have gone through he has never left me.

« CHAPTER 6 »

Aunt Sarah

Soft petals in the wind, someday I know that I will see you again.

As brief as our meeting that's just how it ended.

As inspiration to us all.

With a tear, kind words, honest even hurtful advice.

A hug from you which I still feel will last forever even though you're not here.

Careful pain, for you endured, for those you loved.

Misunderstood just as our Heavenly Father sometimes is from up above.

Like a roller coaster ride our lives were so mysteriously intertwined.

You opened your heart to me without even a question as to how or why.

The love I feel for you will last throughout my life time and more.

For you are more than special, you are a magical, priceless treasure whom I will always adore.

Aunt Sarah made a tremendous impact on my life by showing me a piece of where I came from at one of the lowest points in my life. She loved me when I needed it the most and gave me a priceless treasure that I will forever cherish.

She was full of compassion and good will. She personified strength and had no problems showing it. Unfortunately, she died very soon after I got to know her and it left my heart broken. I still had so much to learn from her about my ancestors. I will forever be in her debt. I miss her dearly and I will always love her.

« CHAPTER 7 »

Behind The Veil

I pray, I beg, I plead, in order to receive divine spiritual-ness to be freed.

Freed from the world as it is in this state; wanting, thirsting, and craving in Jesus name.

Preparing for my journey; delighted, excited, and filled with laughter just at the thought of going home.

But before I can leave this place I must learn to shed the skin that I'm in and operate from my spirit that resides from within.

As I learn this task at hand I become more than an ordinary woman.

I enter into this room filled with spiritual things.

I take a step back in order to receive because I am just utterly dismayed at what my eyes have seen.

This room is not of this world it is of something else and I began to weep at the concept.

I have stepped into another space in time where flesh is not needed and my spirit has taken over my mind.

As I step behind the veil I marvel at the thought of not residing in hell.

As I draw nearer to my goal I began to feel a chill and then I hear a great voice filled with laughter.

So I began to look around and I was amazed at what I'd found behind the veil, oh it was true.

God with his darling son Jesus was waiting with my crew to develop me into this marvelous dimension, yes I am under construction, how about you?

My father and my savior have devised a plan to save my soul regardless of my past plans.

See I have stepped out of flesh and I now operate in spiritual-ness my dear God, oh how I am blessed, to receive your love, grace, mercy, and tenderness in Jesus name, I rest, behind the veil of sheer awesomeness.

Behind the Veil was a poem written after getting a revelation about the three realms of spiritual existence. This is an amazing step to take in your spiritual walk.

I had to learn how to go behind the veil in order to truly get in God's presence. The third realm is where the flesh is not needed, it is a place designed for the spirit where you lose all contact with your human fleshly side and operate from the good God filled Holiness of the third dimension.

« CHAPTER 8 »

Black Love

Come to me my every desire.

Quench my heart which burns of my everlasting desire.

Take hold of my enchanted heart, build my sweetness as I lay down to take part in all that this can be.

Our love for everlasting eternity black love is what I have in thee.

Give me all that you have for me.

Nothing material only truth, love respect, and consistency.

Black love is what I have in thee.

Mold me you, distinctive African man of mine.

Never forget what ultimately define us who we are.

Blackness near even from afar.

Proud of all that I am.

Black love is what I hold in my hands.

Black love is what we share.

Black love common however often thought of as uncommon even rare.

How dare you think such a thing.

For whatever do they mean.

Black love a true African thing.

I have to take it back to our roots.

Please don't be afraid of the truth.

Black love defines us as who we are and who we have always been.

True Kings, Queens, and Warrior men.

Nothing can take that away, as we are greatness in every way.

Yeah! Even till this day.

Black love like this can hear the world.

Just try it, you'll see, so you go girl.

A fact it's good, so don't fear it, get close, go near it.

Black love, it's ours by nature.

Don't hate it just create it.

Black love, can't you hear it, feel it, taste it.

Black love, my people allow yourselves to resuscitate it.

Black Love, I must admit is one of my greatest works. It came at a time when I was in transition. I decided to change my style of writing to that of love instead of pain. I shifted my prospective and chose to see the love that I so greatly desired.

A young lady I knew at the time convinced me to go with her to a poetry show. I was reluctant in the beginning because she informed me that it was also open mic night for all poets. I did not think that I was ready to recite my poetry in front of an audience of people that I didn't know.

Well as fate would have it I decided to go. In the excitement of it all I forgot my book of poems on the kitchen table and didn't realize it until we had already made it to the poetry show. I was devastated. I prepared to miss one of the biggest opportunities of my life until the young lady challenged me by saying, "well you say that you are good, write something now."

I looked at her and said it's only five minutes until show time, how am I going to write something that quick? Besides I don't have any paper. Well she and her friend went into their purses and pulled out some paper and a pen. I then looked around the room and saw my people excited and loving one another, so I put the pen to the paper and gave birth to "Black Love."

« CHAPTER 9 »

Careless

In spite of who I was, despite what I could be, careless is what I am indeed.

Careless to think that I could do two things right.

Careless to think that I could be beautiful in someone else's eyes.

Careless to think that I could be special in a simple day dream.

Careless to think that anyone could truly love me.

Careless to think that I could even be held tight.

Careless to think that he wouldn't ever say goodbye.

Careless to think that anyone would care.

Careless to have held on tight with all my might to someone who never ever could have appreciated me for me.

Careless to have even thought of giving myself to thee.

Careless came at a time in my life when I was again careless and made a mistake that would alter my life forever by not waiting on God to guide me.

Sometimes we as humans tend to think that we are in control of our lives, well that is not true. I know that God does give us options and those are to do right or wrong, there is no in between. We know when things aren't right for us but sometimes we do not want what is right. Oh yes, I did say that.

We are sometimes our own worst enemy and the masters of our self-defeat. I know that very well because many times in my life I have done this very thing to my own self. It is a very disturbing thing to not want to do better because you somehow think that it will not matter.

Certain circumstances can lead us to think that doing good doesn't matter but I am here to let you know that it does matter.

« CHAPTER 10 »

Chaotic

Chaotic is how I feel.

Determined to know the deal.

Of who I am and why I'm here.

Devotion is what I seek along with respect and peace.

Yeah, peace of mine without a dime is like a rhythm without a rhyme.

Controlled by my fears which has turned into days filled with heart ache, pain, and tears.

Chaotic is how I feel.

No one knows because I try not to let it show that I am a walking, talking, shell that feels like I'm already living in hell.

I hear people say, oh girl, you are so strong but they are so wrong.

I be a pillow of worry and grief.

Oh wow, don't sit there in disbelief.

Chaotic do you know her?
Oh, of course, that be me.

Chaotic is a poem that gets you to thinking, why did she write about that? Well the answer to that is very simple to me because I have often felt Chaotic.

When you have done all that you can do and it's not enough. When you have been all that you can be and no one seems to see it, you become fed up with the pressures of life. Chaos is real and it is a terrible state to be in.

I am however very thankful to God that I am not in that state anymore and that I have learned that no matter what I am going through that God sees and he knows. Help is surely on the way when you trust him enough to call out for his help.

I know that God answers cries for help from his children because he has always answered mine. No I am not a religious guru; I am a child of God who trusts in him.

« CHAPTER 11 »

Charisma

Today I prayed, yesterday I stayed, and tomorrow I will say to the one that I love, thank you for entering my world.

You're my gift from up above.

Connecting to you in every way and responsible for the way I feel on this very special day.

Charisma is what I see in you.

Charisma is always trusting in you.

Charisma is a love that's all so emotional and true.

Caring, sharing, and dramatically yours with all thoughts of kindness and sincerely with love.

My everlasting loved one with warmth, generosity, and care.

Come make love to me with such piazza and flare.

Hold me like you've never held anyone before, as if tomorrow does not exist and our love will last forevermore.

As if our survival depended on that lasting and final kiss that will linger with joy and eternal bliss.

As if mankind depended solely on you loving me. As if God prepared me for thee.

As if my soul and yours were combined as one.

As if my eyes shine like the rising of the sun.

As if my smile could launch a thousand ships.

As if you were mesmerized by my curvaceous hips.

Charisma, that word is truly dazzling to me because I think that we all want to possess some sort of charismatic qualities. Charm, flare, and attractiveness all play a key role in this title. I full joyed knowing that someone has a desire for me and considers me to be rather appealing.

What woman wouldn't want to feel that way. It is a part of our human nature. We are very unique beings, all filled with charisma. So tap into yours and full joy what God has created for you. There is nothing wrong with being sensual and alluring.

« CHAPTER 12 »

Chirp, Chirp

Chirp, chirp, the bird sings, flying high, soaring to heaven to hear the angel's sing.

Chirp, chirp, the bird sings preparing for Jesus descending back to earth to claim his prize.

To reign over unbelieving eyes.

Chirp, chirp, the bird sings listening for the bells of heaven to ring.

As loud as a roar of thunder looking down to see what's going on under the clouds a misty blue, gray with streaks, and gleams of white seen from a country or two.

Chirp, chirp, the bird sings waiting for God to send on an assignment of adornment to declare heaven is near and earths in despair, prepare to move up to classroom A and be blessed for everyone will not make it there.

You have finally reached Angel status.

Flap those wings, now come guide us to the pearly gates assigned to me by God, that's a sheer wonder to see.

Chirp, chirp the bird turned Angel has now received those heavenly wings designed to fly to heights that will never be seen.

Chirp, chirp, now listen to that bird truly sing with heavens director and as other angelic voices sing.

Chirp, Chirp is the sound that little birds make. When I am sitting in my car I often look around and watch the birds and sometimes imagine being able to take wings and fly away to heaven singing.

See, to me flying on your own signifies freedom and singing also takes me to a place of solitude. When situations in life become a bit much I often wish that I could fly away. I also envision what my spiritual life will be like when I get back to heaven.

« CHAPTER 13 »

Choir

Chosen to chorus for the Lord's respect.

Honoring him from one day to the next.

Outstanding voices that could wake up the spiritually dead and make them clap, stomp, and rock their heads.

Independently unique in our own rights, some singing soprano, some singing alto, keeping up and staying on key with the piano.

Righteous is he that can sing for thee to put that gospel spell on me.

Oh, I say, choir stand up and sang.

Giving honor to him with that holy name.

Clap those hands.

Stomp those feet.

Send out that message that's wonderfully unique.

That God is alive and he lives inside of me.

Sang that happy song that will shake many nations, making them repent and join us in our song that will last for centuries long.

The choir is set up for our spiritual upliftment, joy, and love.

So full joy this holy gift that we giveth sent from the Lord above.

I say choir sang and show us some love.

Choir was written for the annual choir day at our church. It is an amazing gift to be able to sing praises unto the Lord and show appreciation to God for granting you such a gift. The choir sets the tone for the rest of the service. The music ministry is one of great fulfillment.

« CHAPTER 14 »

Coming Home

Coming home much like coming of age.

Excited, delighted, full of hope and praise.

Coming home to familiar gatherings.

Free to appreciate, dictate, and revelate about things that are yet to come.

Coming home to the eldest ones full of wisdom, joy, and love.

Coming home to teach a few that God is good to both me and you.

Coming home with many memories of what life use to be and how it is today.

Coming home to sing praises to God on this glorious day.

Coming home to rejoice about being blessed yet again.

Coming home much like our ancestors did many years ago.

Once were royalty, then were slaves, now we're celebrating our continued spiritual connection to God with plenty more to gain.

We've come this far through faith by forgiving and remembering from whence we came.

So in a sense coming home means many things but one importantly is that we are all free.

Free to practice being Spiritual out loud.

Free to sing a praise without hiding and being afraid you'd be found out.

Free to teach the young about where we've been.

Free to create that burning passion for God is with me, even if I didn't have neither family nor friends.

Coming home, yes I am blessed to be here again.

Coming Home was written while I was thinking of visiting my birth place. Most people that I have had the pleasure to meet in my life were away from home.

My inspiration was to capture the feeling of returning after being gone for an extended period of time, whether it is family who has moved away many years ago or someone who just went away to college.

The return home can be a very powerful thing and in some instances it can be rather traumatic. We leave home for many different reasons.

Home can have many different meanings as well because many of us are from other countries, islands, states, cities, and rural areas. Going back whether it is permanent or temporary, just do it anyway.

« CHAPTER 15 »

Completion

Completion is the key to put that gospel spell on me. God, man, and woman to me are three hundred and sixty degrees of peace and spirituality.

Anchored at our spiritual survival.

Equip with the tools that we need to defeat our busy enemy.

Undefeated is he that has faith in thee.

Created in his own image, put here on earth to keep peace in his sweet name and grace.

To acquire he wisdom and knowledge that's needed to gain spiritual completion.

Thus to remain undefeated in his holy name.

God is quality control for your souls aimed at both the young and the old.

He is relative to our environment.

Crucial to our element.

Praising him is a must to our daily survival and enrichment.

Working towards a goal where the greatest prize will leave your soul misty eyed.

Rocking the foundation from whence you came making you shout out his holy name.

Completion is the name of this time and it is not a game.

So when the holy one comes he'll be seeking his forever daughter's and son's.

Oh how good is he who lives within me.

Lord, come put that gospel spell on me.

Completion is what I seek in thee.

Completion is the essence of who we are when we truly operate in the will of God.

I know within me I am made whole by the love of God, that resides inside my heart. When I think of the magnificent way in which God has made us in his image it just sends chills through me.

I can put my hand on my chest and fill my heart beating and I know that it is not because I have been so good, but it is because of the power of God.

We as human beings should take the time to notice the tiny ridges on our fingers, the sparkling twinkle in our eyes, and the wrinkles at the edges of our mouth when we smile.

We are amazing because the power of God has completed us, just look around and he will confirm it for you. You are not here by your own accord.

« CHAPTER 16 »

Confusion

Contrary to what we believe confusion is not just a state of mind but a way we live and breed.

On a day to day basis confusion comes and disrupts our lives like a thief in the night waiting to take our pride.

Nevertheless, and needless to say confusion is a distinctive prey.

Furthermore, just to see confusion lurks in our most pleasant of dreams.

Utterly so confusion can be the starter of our self-defeat.

Searching your heart to find the answer to the questions that linger in your mind, then here it comes, confusion.

Indecisive yet transparently so, confusion is an open window on a windy day.

Blowing in particles from near and far.

Confusion, well, well, well, stand up if you have ever been confused. Yes, I wrote a poem about confusion. I wanted others to step back and take a look at just what it is. First and foremost, God is not the author of confusion and he will never lead you astray.

I used metaphors because I wanted to give a clear view as to how quickly we can be pulled off course by life's circumstances.

I know that when you are confused it is because you are struggling with yourself about what you need to do that is right in the eyes of God. Most often we think that doing the right thing will be difficult because that is what being of the world does, but you have to step outside of yourself and still chose to do what is right.

I have many times allowed confusion into my life and had to pay a big price for not making the right choice. I was not trusting myself, therefore I was not trusting God.

« CHAPTER 17 »

Constellation Prize

From the beginning I yearn for the ending of a heart filled with pain.

To step into a world of heartfelt gain.

To be loved by you so effortlessly, continuously, and ultimately free.

To step into a world filled with passion, romance, and excitement.

To learn from the depths of intoxicating and tantalizing love.

To finally feel what it's like to be loved by you so faithfully, committedly, and ever so deservingly.

Take me in your arms and love me from now until infinity.

Constellation prize from God is what you are to me.

With your soul come make love with me and bask in my glow.

POETICALLY ME ♥ 50

Hold me tightly so that I'll know that you're mine and nothing can change that not even time.

Constellation Prize was written during a time of great disappointment for me. It had me wondering why?

Have you ever been so very close to winning something and could feel it in your bones just to have it slip right through your finger's! That's the way that life can sometimes be. You can just know that you have attracted the right person and they turn out to be the wrong one.

Sometimes love isn't even the question at hand, it can be just purely for show, oh, you know what I mean.

Just merely being with someone for the way that they look or because they have a nice ride. In the beginning it feels like you have won the lottery until reality sets in. Whatever the reason being, we know when it is not love.

« CHAPTER 18 »

Content

Do you know what I think about people not reacting to the way that I feel?

I think that they are emotion mutes and can't even handle the deal.

No one seems to relate to the things going on in my life, so I blow up with contempt, anger, envy, and even strife.

Oh, for God's sake, don't sit there with your eyes bugged looking all surprised at me.

I am human and entitled to feel this way.

See, a long time ago I was created from sin and bound from the depths of within.

Always seeking, searching, even preaching to find my place and to no avail I had to give up on that space.

See, life has not allowed me to become who I had hoped, instead I'm here a creature of habit when I should be one of content.

Content with the fact that I am loved and can love back.

Content with the fact that no one, has ever hurt me.

Content with the fact that my reality is not a bad thing.

Content with the fact that today I am really, I mean really free.

Content was written on a day when again things in my life were going so wrong that it become laughable. Who would have even thought that I would be this age and feeling this way.

I have often become sarcastic when things in my life became totally unbearable. That's my way of coping with the things that I can't change.

I am sometimes too honest with my feelings. I have no problem when it comes to expressing how I am feeling whether that is good or bad. I however would love to be content with my life even when it throws me a curve ball.

« CHAPTER 19 »

Daughter of a Drug Addict

It's been too long.

Why can't you stop?

How could this be?

Daughter of a drug addict.

Oh no, not me!

False hopes, broken dreams, confessions of dreadful things.

Daughter of a drug addict.

Oh no, not me!

Night sweats, nightmares, sleeplessly wondering do you care?

That I hurt because of your addiction.

That I cry because of your pain.

That I want you to get help.

That I want you to maintain.

Daughter of a drug addict.
Oh no, not me!

Daughter of a Drug Addict is a controversial topic to say the least and I know that some may be thinking; how could she write that. Well, let's just say that it was not easy. Simply because it is truly a very difficult thing when you have a parent with an addiction and you somehow feel responsible for it.

My mother is a very good person who at the time I wrote this poem had several addictions. I know that a lot of people have this misconception that people who do drug are bad. Well here's a clue, people that do drugs are people who are in a tremendous amount of physiological pain and they need someone to love them in spite of what they are doing.

Don't get me wrong and think that I am saying that you should allow their addiction to be used as an excuse for them to mistreat you. Also, I am not saying that you should be a party to helping them feed their addictions. All I am saying is acknowledge that the addiction exists and try to be supportive when they decide to get help from God.

« CHAPTER 20 »

Devoted

Delivering your undivided attention to me without asking you to.

Handling my heart like God gave it to you.

Concentrating on my every need and always on a mission to please.

Aiming to please my heart on a delicate plain while focusing to maintain.

Accepting me with my flaws and all, in the process of handling me as if I was a precious doll.

Connecting to me in every way and never complaining no matter how long the day.

Releasing your love like God did when he created those delicate white doves.

Have mercy on me, my sweet love.

For I am devoted to you with my heart, mind, soul, and untimely love.

Devoted is a small word that has so much meaning to me because being devoted to someone means that you are willing to accept them with your whole heart.

To make this kind of commitment to a person is an amazing thing. This is clearly what we should do in a spiritual sense as well. Spiritual devotion should come before anything else.

Once you devote yourself to God, then trust that everything else will surely fall into place. I am not saying that once you are devoted that every day will be error or problem free, but no matter what God will surely guide you through the situation and he will allow you to benefit from it.

« CHAPTER 21 »

Does it Ever Get Better?

Does it ever get better?

Does the pain ever go away?

How can one human hurt this way?

The loneliness, the fear, the silence because no one is near.

As the day's pass and I get older, my life gets sadder, my heart grows weaker, my faith has faded, my soul is shaken.

Oh, dear God!

I am tired of waking up to another day of pain, heartache, and nothing to gain.

Does it ever get better? Well I think that this one really speaks for itself. I am not ashamed to admit that sometimes life gets hard for me and yes, I question if it will ever get better. Most of my life has been filled with plenty of pain but I refuse to allow my circumstances to destroy me.

I have realized that I am in a constant battle for my life and this battle includes both good and bad times. I often pray for God to allow me to have more good days than bad and I have faith that my prayers are answered a "yes."

I can truly say that in all that life has brought me God has never left me and he never will. So I have the answer to my question and the answer is "YES!"

« CHAPTER 22 »

Don't Profess/Just Attest

I don't profess to have any doctorates or degrees.

I don't even profess that I am all I that I can be.

All that I can attest to is that Jesus is alive and he resides inside of me.

I don't profess to be a well, known scholar.

I don't even profess to be a well-known author.

All that I can attest to is that Jesus came here and died for me.

I don't profess to be perfect, nor do I even try.

I don't profess to live as other's live their lives.

All that I can attest to is that Jesus and his love will carry me through.

I don't profess to have the master's plan.

I don't even profess to have taken a strong stand for anything righteous in this land.

All that I can attest to is that Jesus is my rock, my fortress, and my foundation.

No matter what occurs bitter or sweet revelations!

My mission is not to hang out with the socially acceptable elite but to be all that my Lord and Savior expects me to be.

My mission is to dwell on God's unchanging words.

To help those who are in need.

To give all that I have in me to him and undertake in spiritual prosperity.

My mission is one that is forever challenging to me because I am to go above and beyond my means.

I am to be what God has willed me to be.

Don't Profess Just Attest is another one of my favorites. You know the love of God is a very powerful thing because he gives us love even when we don't love ourselves.

I often think of the greatest sacrifice that was ever made and that was when Jesus died for our sins. I am often astonished at the thought that he knew what was going to happen before hand and still chose to carry that burden.

I know that compared to Jesus I am nothing and I also know that he loves me in spite of that fact. He does not care that I do not have MD in front of my name. all he wants is for me to maintain a stable healthy relationship with God.

« CHAPTER 23 »

Evolve

Evolve, evolve, into this precious thang.

Evolve, evolve into this miraculous change.

A sense of glory, I am this sensual black woman, for whom I proclaim my dynamic claim to fame.

Fame in which you could never see.

Fame in which only I deem.

Unique, precise, I didn't ask for your advice.

For famous I am in the confines of my mind.

The beauty, the curves, the roundness of my inner mind is so real yet so define.

I am woman, so common to you nevertheless rare and unique to me.

Evolve, evolve with the times of woman for we are all free.

Evolve was written when I was at a point in my life where I was actually comfortable enough to say that I have evolved from that which I was.

Look, if you do not think highly of yourself in this fleshly body then who will. It is okay to feel loved, adored, and respected.

Self-love is the most precious of all because it opens up an unknown world for others to love you as well. I am very thankful that through God's Grace and mercy he has allowed me to be born free.

Now what we do with that freedom is our own choice to make.

« CHAPTER 24 »

Filtered by Flashes

As I drift off to sleep, my body relaxes, my mind clears, my soul steps up and announces that it's here.

It summons my spirit and takes me someplace else.

I am not afraid, although I brace myself.

I hear laughter and my senses heighten as I smell the salt of the ocean breeze, fresh bananas still hidden by the tree leaves.

Papaya's, mango's, and guava's too and that's only to name a few.

Oh, look there it is; as it comes to sight, my place called home under the coolness of the night.

As I settle to place my feet on the sandy beach ground, I can see the lights of the nearby town.

I take a step and hear my name.

I turn towards the voice and I am immediately claimed by my man who shows no shame.

Standing there as handsome "for true!"

Covered by holiness and a garment or two.

He traces the outline of my lips, then kisses me softly as he places a firm yet gentle grasp on my hips.

He lifts me up off of the ground, then spins me round and round.

As the twirls stop I feel anew, oh my, is this what real love will do?

I place both legs around his waist as he prepares to take his place.

My center moistens as it anticipates this grace.

He shifts my weight as he enters the gates of this heavenly space.

With soft moans he tightens his embrace.

As the moves of our dance become intense, he covers my lips with an urgent kiss.

Then whispers in my ear, my darling sweet heart, oh how I've missed this.

He gazed into my beautiful eyes as our holy dance reached peaks, valleys, and astronomical heights.

We climax in unison with sparkles and flares of lights, not from earth but from heavenly sights.

I thrust back and catch a glimpse of heaven filtered by flashes, what's up with this passion.

A chill like no other runs through my veins as I hold on, as I try to maintain what sanity I have left.

Then I catch a flash of something else.

A tear filtered with a smile coming from my man, while he continues to caress me with his strong hands.

As he creatively keeps me suspended in time, I feel as though I have been teleported someplace else, so I began to breathe rapidly, then I hold my breath.

I felt as though I was sinking deeper and deeper into this sea of love, that you would not believe.

As my wonderfully made man thrust's in and out of me.

As we peak, to another high I prepare my soul to say good-bye.

The sweat drips like rain down my lovers back as I scream from sheer pleasure at this uncollated map.

The map is us so perfectly intertwined as we lose ourselves in the suspension of time.

As flashes filtered through our minds, we both awaken after being thrusted in and out, in and out, in and out of time.

We smile just as we always do and grab one another and utter, I Love You, "for true!"

Filtered by Flashes is also included in my list of favorites. It is by far a piece that came to me when I was on a quest to attract the kind of love to me that I knew that I deserved.

It is astonishing what the human mind can come up with when we start to transform ourselves from the old ways of thinking.

We must learn to allow our dreams to manifest themselves into our reality. Never allow anyone to tell you that you are not deserving of the love that you desire.

You must learn to open yourself up to the possibilities that are out there awaiting you because if you want it bad enough it will come.

« CHAPTER 25 »

Get Up Church

Get up let out a mighty roar.

To heaven skies let us soar.

Peace, joy, happiness be still.

No more times to kill.

Where all sickness is healed, so there's no more for pills.

Oh, you don't know the deal.

Get up church, God is real.

To adore, to live for my father whose heaven adorn.

Get up church, raise your hands, clap, shout, and take a stand.

Don't be afraid because God has the plan.

Get up church, give God your hands, while trusting and receiving that Jesus is God's son and right hand man.

Get Up Church is about worshipping God the way that you want to. It is no right or wrong way to praise God.

There are those who tend to condemn others for having their own personal worship experience with God in public.

Your way to praise is just that your way because no one but you truly know just what God has done for you.

Don't be a people pleaser, be God's pleaser. God is the one responsible for your survival not man.

We must realize that the church is us and the church belongs to God. The fact of the matter is everything that we have belongs to God and he so graciously allows us to use it.

« CHAPTER 26 »

Giving Honor to God

Blessed is he that's been called by the Lord to preach his word under a glorious accord.

To teach those among us who aren't aware of God's magnificent flare.

Flare that can change the most impossible of thangs.

Flare that can make even a deaf man sang.

Flare that can make a zillion star's shine so bright, it could give a blind man sight.

Oh, what flare God has there!

To know him in any way will give you too flare on any given day.

So when times are tough and you're filled with despair look up at the sky, that's God's work there.

To treasure, give pleasure, and make you say, oh God, how clever.

Oh, how clever is he that can make any man breathe,

any man Preach, any man teach!

His word so pure.

Oh, how I'm blessed to be filled with his grace.

Touched by his holy place.

Remembering him on every given day.

For blessed is he that gives me peace.

Peace in a world that's filled with his grace.

The type of peace that can soothe a tormented soul.

Peace that makes you feel ten years old.

Peace that dries up those doubtful fears.

Oh, God can give you peace when you're on download, take those painful things and put them on hold.

The type of hold that will make you all feel glad.

Glad to be one of God's children.

Glad to be honoring him and his called one's today in this building.

For blessed is he that knows of thee.

Giving Honor to God is a must. This title says it all because no matter how hard life gets to live, I still have to thank God for allowing me to be a part of it. I often have to give him praise and thanks due to the fact that he has brought me through so much.

Many of you can't even imagine what it's like to be hungry and not have anything to eat. Trust me when I tell you that it is not a good thing. I do not pretend to be anyone other than who I am and I am glad to be in God's good grace because he has touched my heart in a way that I cannot even put into words.

At this point in my life I know that God loves me because I can look back on moments in my life when what I know to be miracles have happened to me. He has saved my life so many times and for that alone I am thankful.

« CHAPTER 27 »

God's Tears

Dripping wet, but not from sweat.

It's heavens rain.

Showering my soul from depth's unknown.

All filled with the holy spirit.

All wide open to swallow more up.

Rain that is too overflow my cup.

The cup is me, can't you see, God's tears falling down on me.

Heaven's up there waiting on me to be filled like that of the mightiest seas.

Oh my, here cometh the holy rain.

Shower me with love from thee, continuously, while walking this earth, I am still free, operating in my secret place, sir named eternity.

So I say, here cometh the rain on me over shadowing everything here that's meant to be.

Just not the greatest creation which just so happens to be me.

Loved by he, him in me.

All I am is who he has me to be.

Shower your blessings down on me.

Heaven's rain can't you see, their God's tears cleansing your soul thus making you free, to operate from heaven while being on earth temporarily.

God's tears, please come touch me.

God's Tears came along at a time when I was at yet again another crossroads in my life.

What a miracle it is to have God cry with you, for you and on you. That to me is amazing. God is a loving God who does weep for his children. He wants us to want him just as he wants us.

It took me a long time to learn that God is here for me no matter what and once you feel God's touch, you will never be the same.

« CHAPTER 28 »

Gravitating to Freedom

How dare you pull me to this earth and leave me here then laugh and say, you have nothing to fear.

Oh, but I do and I feel so out of touch and confused.

Eager to please you at all cost but afraid to for fear of being left out and even lost.

The coordinates of my area are too literal for me to believe.

I wonder around asking myself how could all this be?

I am nothing, a nobody, how can this task be for me?

I can't leap over mountains.

I can't dive salty seas.

I am no one, just look at me.

A child of yours full of hope, despair, love, and grief.

Who told you to just up and leave me?

You said to be in the world and not of it, but it has dragged me kicking and screaming and begging to be released.

I want to be free!

Free to love without being lost.

Free to move without penalty cost.

Free to laugh without being accused.

Free to live without being misused.

Free to linger within the confines of my mind without losing space or time.

Free to travel outside my own boundaries.

Free to write something just for me.

Free to rhyme the words longitude and latitude without being called ridiculous or even rude.

Free to leave this atmosphere and gravitate to places unknown.

Free to color my house black, then call it my home.

Free to be held down by love and not by life.

Free to have a thought without anyone else wondering why.

Freedom at what cost?

How can this be?

I thought slavery ended.

This can't be me.

Shackled by chains, linked by words, confused by dreams, shattered by dreadful things.

Gravity took a hold of me and I don't like it, please let me float free.

Into a place filled with only good things, where no children lie, die, or worry over anything.

A place of peace, filled with sweet nothings, and Godly things.

Gravitating to Freedom came to me in my dreams and I know what you are thinking. How dare she. Who does she think she is? Well, I am a child of God who likes to have conversations with him often and sometimes those conversations are very much like this one in gravitating to freedom.

I love God and I know that he loves me and yes I question my existence here on this earth. I am here on this planet by God's will and not my own. I am honest enough to say that sometimes my conversations with God are intense.

« CHAPTER 29 »

Gravity

Life is just an illusion of painful meaningless mishaps that often occur.

It's like gravity in its present state here on earth and then you leave orbit and enter into space.

Life all of a sudden becomes weightless as all the problems of everyday living seem to subside.

Happiness returns along with joy and soon I become misty eyed at the thought of not ever hurting again and the complications of circumstances never breaking my spirit from within.

Away goes self-pity and meaningless pride.

I finally have arrived at a place where nothing matter's and everything's alright.

It's a place full of delight where gravity doesn't hold you down and I am floating weightlessly like a breath of air flowing oh so free, of course to heaven and it doesn't matter what you think of me because I have arrived at a place where I am finally not a controversy and all filled with hate.

Alone I am able to create, respond, and reflect about what I've done right instead of all I've done wrong.

A home where positivity even radiates from my stride and I have a glow that would wake up the blind.

I am standing a long side all the things I have taken out of my insides that were keeping me bound and put them in a bag to bury so that they will never again be found.

I am no longer a slave to gravity, I am weightless floating forever free and no longer a captive to misery.

Gravity a title that I was very reluctant to write about but a higher power told me to use it anyway. So that just proves that when you listen to God you do not always get to do what you want to do but he always has your best interest at heart.

I have a problem sometimes with being hard headed. I was told to start this poem many days before I actually did because I just could not see pass the title.

What would I write about gravity? And what does that have to do with my life. Little did I know that my entire life had everything to do with the gravitational pull that controls my very existence.

« CHAPTER 30 »

He

He may not have been who you wanted him to be.

But he was a man who wanted his soul just to be free.

A man faced with trying to extend for the purpose of remaining a constant from within.

A man who didn't know who he faced in the mirror each day.

A man full of rage who just wanted to break away.

A man troubled by the mistakes that he made.

Enslaved by the thoughts of never trying to refrain.

Running, hiding, trying to escape from the unknown that lingered within.

So much so that he left a trail of hurt that became his constant friend.

However, through the hurt, pain, and anguish of wanting to be free.

He found a friend that just so happen to be me.

He confided in me a secret that I now must share.

He was sorry for the hurt, pain, and anger that he shared.

However, he wants you to leave all those gifts in a place for no one else to share.

A place so far from anywhere you can conceive so that the rest of our generation can be freed.

He by far was very confusing for me to write about. I never thought that I would ever get to know this man. He ended up being a life lesson for me.

He has had a tremendous impact on my life. I learned that had I known him sooner I would have been a more pain filled person.

See, I walked around wearing this banner of regret because I didn't know my family and I always felt that if I had known them then my life would have somehow been complete, well I was wrong. I was taught a very painful lesson about family and their legacies.

« CHAPTER 31 »

Heart Full

Heart full of laughter.

Heart full of love.

Heart full of bountiful things.

That's what I'm thinking of.

Heart full of grace.

Heart full of faith.

Heart full of compassion.

Heart full of impeccable taste for Jesus to fill up all of my voided space and create a new me in his name, for God's sake.

See, the evolution of man depends upon this to break the chains of lost innocents.

To strive for Godliness is what I seek, never ignoring the holiness that lies within me.

Telling me to do well and loving me from within, comforting me and being my best friend.

Reassuring me with plenty of heartfelt love.

Connecting me with the holy spirit and guiding me through this world with a heart full of agape love.

Heart Full was written from the prospective of being filled with all of the goodness that God gives. There is nothing more sacred than the love that God so graciously gives to us and he interns expects us to allow the love that he shows us to be shown to others.

With all the twists and turns that life sometimes throws upon us, we must do our best to keep our hearts full of God.

« CHAPTER 32 »

How Bout

How bout I take you from all the stresses of life.

How bout I buy you something nice.

How bout I take you to get your nails done.

How bout I take you south to see your son.

How bout I take you to my bedroom and fill you up with babies, then leave you to care for them all alone.

How bout I steal your money, car, and pride.

How bout I take you on one of life's hardest rides.

How bout I tell you I love you just to see the look on your face.

How bout I screw someone else while you're at work in your home and personal space.

How bout I use you until there's nothing but regret written all over your face.

How bout was written at a point in my life when I was disappointed about the decision to allow another person in. my life during the painful process of getting to a point to love again and then be betrayed is not an easy thing to cope with. So I turned to my pen and paper for comfort and clarity.

« CHAPTER 33 »

How Can You Dare to Dream?

Who told you that you had a place?

A place in this world so full of disgrace.

You dare to dream of better things.

A life full of pain and no one cares.

Who's the blame?

A tear, a sigh, a wonder why?

Oh God, why am I so afraid to cry?

The piercing pain that still remains, in my heart that's full of shame.

Shame to dream of a better place.

Shame to invade someone else's space.

Alone again, alone again.

When does this all end?

How Can You Dare to Dream was written at a point in my life when I felt like giving up on my dreams because they appeared to be unreachable.

I have often heard in my life that anything worth having is often hard to obtain.

Through my circumstances I have been forced to face the fact that my dreams had not become a reality because I was not applying myself in the proper manner nor had I been putting forth the time required.

« CHAPTER 34 »

I Am Woman

Hey women stand up, shout aloud I am woman, strong, mighty, and proud.

Pride that would raise a many days of sunshine on even the darkest haze.

Mighty enough to push a freight liner down the largest sea and never break my stride along the way.

Strength that could bench press thousands of screaming kid's without breaking a nail or losing the glow of her skin.

Woman, amazing and unique from the depths of her soul within.

Not one day, two days, or even three.

I am woman giving my all from now into infinity.

Women look, can't you feel me.

See, when everyone else is asleep, we are ironing, cooking, cleaning, and trying to find free!

Yeah, you know free.

Free to take a shower without counting down.

Free to paint your nails without having to frown.

Free to curl your hair without holding your breath.

Free to drive the carpool without losing yourself.

See, freedom is what we seek while trying to save our children from defeat.

I am Woman is a poem written because we as women do not stop to take the time to acknowledge just how unique we truly are.

We get so caught up in our daily duties that we don't take the necessary time to renew ourselves.

Ladies where would your families be if you cease to exist?

Take the time required to nurture yourself and give the adequate time to God for the renewing process to be effective.

You can't truly teach others if you aren't aware of who you are first.

« CHAPTER 35 »

I Got the Gift

I got the gift embedded deep down in my soul and it will never leave me even when I grow old.

I got the gift, the greatest one of all, it keeps your spirit filled even in the worst fog.

I got the gift, can't you see it rising oh so high like the great sparrow gliding up in the sky.

I got the gift, the greatest one of all, to feel the love of Jesus even when I look defeated by all.

I got the gift indeed and it's really true, see Jesus he died not just for me but also for you.

I got the gift the greatest one of all, it picks me up every time that I fall.

I got the gift and it will never lead me astray.

I got the gift living in me every minute of every day.

I got the gift down to the marrow in my bones leaping and jumping for joy when I conquer my fears and practice not doing wrong.

Oh I got the gift, the greatest one of all, its Jesus blood on the cross dripping down covering me, protecting my soul and allowing me to be free.

Oh I got the gift, can't you see it in me!

I Got the Gift sounds like I am bragging about my God given abilities as a poet and I am. I know that all that I write is because God allows me to do so.

This gift of writing was so graciously given to me by God. I am nothing without God and I know that and I am not afraid to acknowledge that.

God uses me as one of his many vessels and I am even amazed at what ends up on my paper when I finish writing.

I thank God for loving me so much that he allows me to write his words.

« CHAPTER 36 »

I Said

I said that I'd love you forever, I think not.

I said that I'd be with you no matter whatever, I think not.

I said that you were my best ever, I think not.

I said that I wanted you to be my man always, to marry me, and allow me to have your babies, I think not.

I said that you were my soul mate sent down to me from heaven, I think not.

I said that I could not imagine my life without you, I think not.

I said that I know what you want and I know what you need.

It's me baby!

I think not.

I said that I would not judge you by your past, I think not.

I said that I would never give your love a try, I think not.

I said I would never say good-bye.

Why I can't believe that I told that lie.

I Said is a small title with a big topic. The power of the tongue is a mighty thing and a truly amazing power that our mouth possesses.

I have learned that it is not what goes into the mouth that defiles it but rather what comes out of it. I have learned also that success and failure are in the power of our words.

I know that many are skeptical about what I am saying but all you have to do is try it out because if you keep talking negatively to yourself then surely negativity will follow and the same applies for positive thinking as well.

We must first think that we can do something good and then we will take the necessary steps to ensure that it happens.

I can clearly look back on events in my life when I defeated myself by doubting my ability to carry out the task at hand.

We must at all times reassure ourselves with positive thinking, then follow it up with plenty of positive speaking.

« CHAPTER 37 »

Kitti

Do you like I do me!

Born into a supreme identity.

Uniquely made with the thickness of a hot babe.

Thick thighs, full hips, and energy forever with juicy lips.

Juiciness, dripping wet, come on let kitti be your pet.

Stroke her, kiss her, make her smile, and watch her purr out loud.

(Growl)

Oh don't stop now, let me instruct you how.

Stroke her hair, part her lips, kiss her gently on her clit.

Oh that's it, don't stop now.

You've just started, work that mouth.

Gently glide that magical tongue.

Watch out now, you gone make Kitti cum.

Put that I on my G.

Don't worry about the time, for we have no need. Swirl that tool with a clock wards groove.

Slow down now, don't rush this Boo.

Taste that spot, don't you stop.

Kitti gone cum, watch out now.

Oh yeah, oooo that's it, stroke that Kitti, oooo work that clit.

Swirl that tongue, wrap it round.

Kiss that clit, oooo watch out now.

Round and round with a magical motion.

Kitti gone cum, oooo get ready for her potion.

Don't stop work that tongue, watch out now, oooo Kitti gone cum.

Up and down, round and round, Kitti's flamin' hot, just see how.

Work that tongue, part those lips, grab those hips, lick that clit.

Round and round, up and down, Kitti's gone cum, oooo watch out now.

Savor the flavor, don't you stop.

Working Kitti is a full time job.

Lick them walls, grip them thighs, lift them cheeks, oooo oh so high.

Up and down, round and round.

Oh tonight Kitti's gone clown.

That tongues tight, oooo that's it Boo.

Poetry in motion, bodies strokin', Kitti's purrin', love juices flowin'

Oh "my my" oooo grab that thigh.

Open me up boy. I'm about to fly, to another land.

Come on Boo, lick that Kitti, don't stop, oooo.

I'ma grab them dreads, oooo pump that head.

Lick that clit, get well fed.

Round and round, up and down, it's jumpin' off, way down town.

Work that body, caress my knees.

Oh baby, don't stop please.

Here I go, yeah again.

Kitti's gone cum, yo tongue her best friend.

In and out, out and in.

I'm a scream, you're a ten.

Kitti's happy, how about you?

Wait a minute, I'm not through.

Just getting started, don't you quite.

Kitti's greedy, she likes to be licked.

Up and down, round and round.

Kitti's ready to throw down.

Now flip me over, on my side, lift my leg, way up high, to the sky, I'ma star, watch me shine, dip in far.

Way down deep, past the wall, oooo don't let, that leg fall.

Hold it up, keep it straight, stretch that tongue through my gate.

Oooo yeah, oh that's it.

Work that tongue, on my clit.

Oooo, oooo, you gone make me act a fool.

Up in here, oh my dear.

Break me off, some of that.

Here comes Kitti, your purring Kat.

She has the flavor of a berry.

Come on Boo, work that cherry.

Oh don't stop, don't you quite.

Work that Kitti, but not too quick.

Round and round, up and down.

Lick that Kitti, like you a hound.

Bury that face, in my bound.

Oh yeah, oooo that's it.

Work that kitti, don't you quite.

You're my Boo, I'm your babe.

Keep licking that Kitti, don't be afraid.

Round and round, up and down,

Oooo yeah, what out now.

I'ma cum, oooo whew, tasty ha.

My bodies jerkin'.

My toes are curling.

Your tongues a swirlin'.

Your lips are kissin'.

Keep it comin', ain't nothin' missin'.
Rotate my hips, gyrate like that.
Up and down, oooo round and round.
Lick that kitti, you makin' her proud.
In and out, out and in.
Oooo whew, I did it again.

Kitti may actually be my most controversial poem to date because of the graphic yet sensual concept of it.

There are some who would say that since I am a minister that I should not be thinking let alone writing such a poem.

Well, let me set the record straight, my poem Kitti is no more sensual or graphic than the book of Song of Solomon in the bible.

Yes, I said it. Now let that sink in for a minute. Especially for the bible scholars out there.

Listen, just because I happen to be a servant of God doesn't mean that my desires have been cut off. God placed these desire within me and God also gave me the knowledge required to write this poem.

I will never deny that I am a spiritual being patterned after God's own heart and I am also happy to say that God indeed made me this way.

« CHAPTER 38 »

Let Me!

Let me love you the way that no other can.

Stretch fourth your arms and take hold of my hands.

Summon your spirit to connect too mine.

Let down your guard and be controlled by time.

Allow Love to take over your flow and give chance to romance in a way that you've never know.

Command my lips to allure you and tantalize.

Let my heart take over your mind.

Love me my dear sweet, from now, until the infinity of time.

Let Me! Just so happens to be a poem about allowing yourself to be totally engulfed in love in a way that it draws you closer to God and makes you strive to be the best you that you can be no matter what anyone else thinks.

It is a shame that on the flip side of this spectrum that some people are so broken that you have to convince them to even allow you to love them.

« CHAPTER 39 »

Life

Life as it is, is what we remember.

The sacrifices we make,

The hard knocks we take.

Life as it is, is what we believe.

That good times are few and far between.

That bad times are plenty and come too often.

That sooner than later that we all will end up in coffins.

Life as it is, is what we conceive.

As our mind thinks.

As our heart beats.

As our bodies breed.

Life as it is, is what we see.

A child being shot down on the city's streets.

A moment in time when we notice that our grass is green.

A mother turned dope fen, selling her body for a fix.

Life as it is, is what we can't overstand.

The killing of our people with no remorse or fear.

The massive diseases that plague us here.

The family structure gone but not forgotten, as they live on the streets and eat from garbage's.

Life is about truth. The truth that there are moments in my life when I get fed up and being able to admit it. Whether it be on paper or out loud.

Yes, life can become very depressing when you are overwhelmed by the news and other programs that focus on the negativity in the world instead of the positivity.

I know that life can get hard to deal with at times because of the circumstances that we as people sometimes find ourselves in.

I am thankful to God for giving me the gift to express my feelings on paper because writing for me is a stress reliever as well as a comfort zone.

I overstand that no matter what life throws my way I can rely on God's grace to get me through it.

« CHAPTER 40 »

Lord's Supper

For I say unto you this supper marked the beginning of a beginning for mankind.

It opened up our eyes and allowed us to see the unbelievable.

To encounter, witness, and conceive the truly amazing.

For the Lord laid down his life for thee.

By doing so he allowed my soul to be born free.

He broke bread at that table knowing that there sitting with him was an enemy.

However, he showed great strength at that meeting and did what was asked of him to save our people.

The Lord's supper truly a moment in time to be cherished.

For breaking bread, which is the bread of life.

For drinking wine, which is the blood of Christ.

Gives true meaning to the word we will call life.

The Lord's supper is more than just a moment in time that fulfilled the human desire to eat.

It's a moment in time when the Lord showed great submission and did his father's will in order to make our lives complete.

Lord's Supper was written because every time I think of the way that Jesus must have felt at that moment in his life, I gasp because I know for a fact that I am not that strong.

Some people have wished that they could know what's going to happen next in their lives but I am not one of them.

To know ahead of time what life brings you next must be very a very painful thing. I say this because not all things are good just as all things are not bad and having that knowledge to know beforehand could bring about total destruction to not only the one who knows but to others as well.

This just proves that we all have a purpose in life and we can either have a negative or a positive impact on generations to come.

« CHAPTER 41 »

Mother

A mother is always there for you.

A mother is always true to you.

A mother is what I see in you.

A mother is precious because she gives us life.

A mother is the sunshine that lights up our lives.

A mother can be many things; courageous, caring, loving, and dedicated to you.

A mother builds up her child with hopes and dreams.

A mother sheds tears for you over the slightest of things.

A mother prays for her child to be all that he or she can be.

A mother loves you from the depths of her heart.

A mother is to be appreciated in a way that you could never imagine.

Someday, someway, Mother I want you to see just how much you have touched my heart eternally.

Mother is a poem that really doesn't need an explanation as to why it was written. Each of us on this planet has a mother and she means different things to different people.

However, as I sit back and think of all the women who haven't given birth, I say to you, don't fret because if you have been around other people's children and nurtured and loved on them then you are too a mother.

I know that it doesn't take the place of giving birth to your own child but please don't minimized the fact that you being present in a child's life, that needs you, is still Mothering.

« CHAPTER 42 »

My Christmas Wish

I didn't wish for fancy cars, a nice house, or a rich man, all I've ever wished for was the family I've never had.

Growing up with a so called family full of drugs, alcohol, and abuse, there's nothing I'd like to see more than a mother rejoicing over the joy of her son's voice.

Her eyes filled with tears as the holiday comes because her house is filled again, then it becomes a home.

As I am a person so alone, trying to break the cycle of a broken home.

Bearing the pressure of making the change; caressing, connecting, feeling the pain.

Being alone is nothing like being lonely.

When you're lonely you have someone to call but when you're alone there's no one at all.

Oh, how I wish for what you have, a mother to be with, a helping hand.

Someone to call to say, "Guess what Mom?"

"I love you more because you're my closest thing to God."

Oh yes, I know that life is full of up's and downs but having a family picks you up and puts you on the rebound.

When I need someone I turn to me because I'm my only family.

Being close to someone is something that I've never had, that's why I love my son with all the strength that I have.

All I think about is giving him the things that I've never had, the love, the joy, the finesse of being glad; glad to be a part of his mother's life.

When he's around everything's alright.

I don't want fortune, glamour, or fame, all I want is to help myself maintain; my two-part family which is all that remains and I'm so proud that Jeffrey is his name.

With love from a friend.

I'm sorry that this Christmas didn't bring you a material thing from me, only my warmth and kindness from the heart definitely.

Merry Christmas to you from my only point of view.

My Christmas Wish is another one of my favorites, written during a time when I was young and transitioning.

Have you ever been in a place in your life where you thought that everything around you was wrong? Well I have and this poem led me to wish for what I did not at the time have.

I was not close with my family and we all had our own pain to deal with which left us separated.

I would see other families positively interacting with one another and I wanted that. I felt as though I was stuck in a family that did not know joy, happiness, peace, prosperity and most importantly love.

I was overwhelmed by the holidays and wanted very much for my son Jeffrey to have all the things that I did not, but my task was not as simple as having money, I needed God in my life.

I needed to accept my circumstances and do my part to make it better. Thus in doing better I would break the chains that was placed upon my family long before I was born.

By having an active and healthy relationship with God I could better myself and therefore help others. I am a living witness that God can turn your bad into good.

Trusting in him and knowing that no circumstance will last always and just because it appears that you do not have something now does not mean that you will not have it later.

« CHAPTER 43 »

My Father's Love

Nobody can love me like my father can.

He stretches out his arms and gives me his hands.

Then he guides me through my day to keep me from harm's way.

He walks me through life with patience and he overstands that I am his, no matter where I stand.

He knows that I will make mistakes but he gives me the opportunity to try again.

As long as I repent and trust that he has no limits and that he loves me.

He's at the side lines cheering me on, hoping that I win by remaining strong.

However, if I fail at the task at hand he will leave the side lines just to give me his hands.

He will then pick me up and wish me good luck.

If I need a pep talk he will give me that and also if I need a pat on the back.

He showers me with plenty of love.

Like when he allows me to breathe his air, that's so sweet.

Or when he allows me to see the world he made, that's all so unique.

Oh, I know that my father loves me.

He accepts me for who I am with all my flaws.

He's my number one man because nobody can love me like my father can.

When everyone leaves me and goes on their way my father remains with me no matter the time of day.

He comforts me, keeps me, and allows me to be free.

He gives me that special kind of love that he knows that I am worthy of.

The kind of love that will leave your soul dancing until it's old.

And when it's old and all filled with the spirit that he gives, he'll whisper and say come home my dear child because today is your day.

Just in case you don't know my father, the one that I am speaking of, his name is Yahweh and he always gives me plenty of love.

My Father's Love was by far one of my favorite topics to write about. It is one of the greatest honors in this world to be loved by God.

Nothing and I mean nothing compares to the love that only God can give because it is Agape.

The kind of love that touches your spirit and leaves you changed forever.

« CHAPTER 44 »

Our Love

Leap into the windows of my soul as my heart, mind, and body unfold.

Into this miraculous creature I've become, as we intertwine and emerge as one.

As green as the grass can be my love for thee, is that in which we can't see.

For I can only imagine the depths of ecstasy we uncover this evening.

As we lose ourselves in the pleasures of the seasons; for love there need not be any other reason.

A soft whisper from you in my gentle ear is all I want for when you're not near.

I can see your face in my mind as it is sketched and nothing can remove it not even time.

As we grow old, nothing can move me like the way you can touch my soul.

Not even death, for I know that's not the end of it all.

For after death our spirits will live on and for we will love together each other all eternity long.

A gift we share so obvious, however so unfortunately rare.

For living without each other is like taking a breath without air.

Our Love was of course written about the love between a man and a woman.

That kind of love should be one of the most awesome things on this planet, however it does not always work that way.

I know that in order to fully love anyone you must first love yourself and when you truly love yourself it shows in everything that you do, especially in the choices that you make.

I am one to admit that at one point in my life I did not love myself the way that I should have. I made choices that showed that I did not love myself properly.

When you make the choice to be in relationships that you know is bad for you, that is not love but rather self-loathing.

I would often write about truly loving someone because that is what I really wanted, although I knew in my heart that that is not what I had. It wasn't until I fully accepted God and realized that in order to be a recipient of love you must possess the gift of being able to give love.

Learning to love was a very painful process for me because I harbored so much anger and resentment that it took many life lesson in order to release all of that.

« CHAPTER 45 »

Pray Up

When life gets too hard for you to live, that's when you pray up.

When troubles from your life stop you from getting out to fellowship, you pray up.

When the pain of life gets too hard to bare, you pray up.

When you look around and all you see are Satan snares, you better pray up.

Pray to God who is your only way.

The one who will keep you no matter the time of day.

Oh, he's the one to put you back on the right track, setting your feet on solid ground.

Helping you to choose to live and strengthening you to fight another round.

Put on your battle gear and allow him to prepare you for the end is near.

There will be no more burdens to bare, soon you'll be full of laughter instead of despair.

Oh, I know you're thinking who am I to tell you this.

Well, I am one of God's children, can't you picture it?

I am only one of many and he still manages to hold my hand when I need to be guided.

He still manages to lift me up on my down days to look over the horizon.

He still manages to rock me like I'm his only baby when my soul is crying.

See, I don't care what you think of me because I am a living witness that God's my father and he wants better than this for me

Pray Up was written when I decide one morning instead of focusing on all the negative that was surrounding me that I would instead focus and pray for the positive.

I thought about all that was happening to me and I became sad. It really seemed as if I was fighting a losing battle. But that is not even the worst of it, I looked as if I was fighting a battle all alone.

Then God reminded me that I was not fighting alone because he was in fact fighting for me.

It is very hard to see that when you are bombarded by so many of life's challenges all at once.

I found myself constantly losing focus and dwelling on the problems instead of the solutions.

« CHAPTER 46 »

Released

As my mind drifts into an area usually untapped.

I gaze into my spirit at this unclaimed map.

It's filled with all sorts of things, but one in particular a love never before seen.

A love that has surpassed the era of time, marked by signals of an eternal kind.

My soul has claimed this priceless treasure of rare and unique pleasure.

Released by a key of everlasting unity of my spirit untold.

Grab ahold of my heart and never let go.

Connected by our spirits from deep within.

Loving from the third dimension, transformed by God's kin.

Made for me and I for you, released by God to reunite us in a cue.

A cue called this world tapped into our minds, lead together by our spiritual maps, controlled by no mankind.

A union released by God from above, created with splendor of unforsaken love.

Controlled by a signal of spiritual depth.

Trying to hide from the world this unspoken rift.

While our love radiates from this spiritual cliff.

A love so clear and yet unseen.

Packed with a punch of terror as if in a dream.

Magnetized by all that I am.

While cleaving to all that you are.

Searching depths never near, always those afar.

Our love rare as unimagined magic from unearthly dimensions.

Transformed by God's clearest intentions.

Released by spiritual directions while clinging to God's connections.

Come love me like never before throughout eternity and forevermore.

Priceless treasure guided to me by a spiritual map, etched in my heart directly from heaven.

Hold my hand my special made man who will always show me that he can love me from the map of especially made plans.

Released by love because I know that I am.

Released is about love and the abundance thereof. The true joy and acceptance that comes from the anticipation of having that one and only one that God created you to be with.

It is a joining of not just the bodies but more so the spirits. It is a fulfilling of the yearning that we have when we are not connected to the other part of ourselves.

« CHAPTER 47 »

The Power of the Mist

In the mist of the evening when you're away.

I can feel your presence and smell your scent, one in which you can only carry that way.

I long for you in a way that is mysterious even till this day.

The way you walk, talk, and yes smell, takes my body through an emotional whirl.

On those days when we're together, I take long looks into those beautiful eyes and I'm taken on a magical ride.

Into a world only you can take me to.

One without a name, where there's no need for a bus, plane, nor train.

A place where there's only me and you, living with a love that's unbelievable yet true.

A love that takes my breath away.

Just thinking of it gets me through the day.

I imagine your smile and it sets me all aglow.

Your graceful touch, the way you make me float, no raft needed, not even a boat.

For with a love like this is all I need sealed with that luscious kiss.

Oh baby, don't you feel it? You know, the mist.

Oh the ambiance you use could light up a room.

Your style, your grace, the smile you put upon my face.

Oh baby, I know, that you know, what you do to me.

I sat aside my lady like manner and take on the personality of a gorgeous black panther.

I glide, I swerve, I entice you with the movement of my curves.

From the roundness of my behind, the softness of my back, the fullness of my hips, even the way I lick my lips are some of the things that turn you on.

Oh baby, don't you feel it? You know, the mist.

The Power of the Mist is of course on my favorites list because of the amazing way in which God so graciously gave it to me.

It is about the power of the smell. Yes, the way a person smelled moved me to write one of my greatest poems.

The impact of that beautiful aroma was so profound that hours later I could still smell it while taking my bath.

The smell compelled me to jump out of my tub and grab a pen and some paper, jump back in the tub and create one of my master pieces.

I am still in awe at the beauty of the piece and the magnificent power of God.

« CHAPTER 48 »

Today God Spoke to Me

Today God spoke to me through a gracious and meek man.

Who just so happen to tell me of his plan.

His plan to deliver me from all my pain filled years.

To help me rise above the occasion and help me forget those bitter revelations.

Oh what joy I felt as tears swell up my eyes.

I looked with amazement as to how and why.

I had to ask and it was given.

God came to me straight from the heavens and put his holy spell on me.

Now my heart is filled with hope instead of grief.

Oh God, thank you for giving me so much peace.

Today God Spoke to Me was graciously given when I was again at a crossroad in my life and of course again seeking direction and clarity about some things.

I can overstand a person's reaction to this because a lot of people think that when you talk about God talking to you that you must be automatically crazy or mentally challenged, if you will.

Well, I am neither and I know that God has his ways of communicating with us. It is however up to each individual to overstand and know when God is speaking.

« CHAPTER 49 »

Two Way Remembrance

I know that if all of us would take a moment to reflect back on our lives, we all could think of several people who in some way have touched our hearts that we've lost.

Gone but definitely not forgotten!

Remembered with laughter and plenty of heartfelt I gotcha's!

In remembrance to those we have loved, missed kisses and long soulful hugs.

Gone but not forgotten to those of whom we have adored.

Thankful for those who we have lost because they have somehow showed us how to love.

For without love our lives would be meaningless.

Love is truly a blessing from the Lord up above.

Love is indeed the key to everything that life is and will ever be!

Gone but not forgotten as your faces will forever be sketched in our memories.

Life's funny like that when we search our hearts to find fun filled memories of those who have left us behind.

But before we fret and shed sorrowful tears.

Rejoice and be thankful for those times we have shared here.

For here is just temporary, like a bus stop on our summer trip.

For our final destination is heaven, so hold on my dear.

Blessed we are to have met down here.

To have shared a stroll by the lakeside or the birth of our first child.

Blessed again to have known one of God's prodigy's.

So we'll throw up our hands in heaven as we say, hay!

I knew that I would see you again someday!

Then we'll stroll along as if we have never left one another's side and never again worry of anything else breaking our stride.

In remembrance to those who have left us behind.

As we take a breath and look up in the sky we can see your faces and immediately know why just the mere thought of you all makes us glow in the night.

See you all were Angel's masquerading as simple humans in our eyes.

Two Way Remembrance came to me after another death in my family. The death caused me to write a poem about the remembering of those that are no longer on this planet in a physical sense.

This poem looks at both sides of death. I had to touch on the fact that not only do we grieve for our loved ones but we also want to know that they have crossed over into heaven.

I know that it gives comfort to those who have lost loved ones for a specific reason and no I do not know what God's reasons are but I do know that we all complement one another and that when someone enters our lives it is to teach us something about ourselves.

« CHAPTER 50 »

Two Way Remembrance (Response)

Oh, Angel's we are indeed, so prepare to receive.

Stretch out your arms as far as you can reach, with a smile on your face because I know that you can see me.

I am who I am.

As I was all that I could be.

So please do not frown at the thought of not being with me.

For as sure as I am that you know that God is our creator and Jesus died on Calvary.

Surely we will reunite in heaven where we will live throughout eternity.

So I say, stretch out your arms and come greet me.

Full of laughter and love, not a tear of sorrow in my eyes.

I tell you heaven is much more debonair than being on the other side.

As I take a sigh and look around me.

I can see bountiful mountains, crystal clear seas, and a sight you wouldn't believe.

It's my father in heaven standing right here in front of me.

I declare that he is truly God indeed.

So do not fret my dear, I am fine up here.

Just remember me and all that I was there.

Smile at the thought that my memories will forever linger like those ridges on your finger or the grayness of your hair or even the strut in your stride.

For I will forever be the apple in your eyes and nothing can surpass that, not even time.

Two Way Remembrance (Response) is the second part of Two Way Remembrance. This is the transitioned loved one's response to the grieving family members.

It is a detailed conversation about how they would feel about their own death and also being a comfort to the love ones that have been left behind to deal with the loss.

« CHAPTER 51 »

Unity

Unity in numbers can rock a troubled foundation.

Unity in number is the key to our spiritual salvation.

Unity, progress, and adversity can stop; anger, betrayal, and strife.

Unity in our community can deter any negative plan.

For God is the master of this time we have at hand.

Love coupled together we can go down in history as freedom fighters in God's army.

Honoring and protecting those which came before us.

Providing a stable and steady foundation for our freedom fighters of tomorrow.

For in our quest to honor God we must examine what we stand for.

For if we stand for nothing prepare to fall for anything.

Receive him, our Lord and Savior first above all others, then we as a people become unstoppable on our pathway to righteousness.

Our history is a priceless treasure for which it should be honored and taught on a daily basis.

So that our future generations become equip with the knowledge needed to keep our heritage alive.

So strive for unity under God's protective plan.

As we venture on with our daily lives remember what Malcolm, Martin, Medgar, and many others stood for.

Acknowledge and cherish the freedom that God allows us to have, paid for by the blood of our Savior.

Black History ours today, tomorrow, and forever.

Unity is a subject matter that we as a people still struggle with. I had always been told that united we stand and divided we fall but through many painful life lessons I have discovered that to be not true.

Unity is a very powerful thing because two or three joined together in Jesus name can change so many things.

All it takes is one person to get another one to listen and react. God can gather together his flock and oh my, look at what can happen.

I do not doubt the power of God because I know that he is mighty indeed. He can pull us together and he can also separate us.

I have learned to put my relationship with him first because he is the glue that holds everything together whether you want to give him the credit or not.

I know that God wants us to unite and serve him as a whole family going to worship and serving him together. Praying and thanking him for allowing us to be a part of the heaven on earth, that he created.

« CHAPTER 52 »

Upward Bound

I am upward bound see me climb.

I am now free to be all that I did not know how.

On earth I did all that I could do and my reward is Heaven and it's glorious too.

No more battle's, no more tears of sorrow in my eyes, for I am a warrior that has just broken my earthly stride.

Don't feel bad for me because I have arrived at a place you should someday hope to be.

I am upward bound can't you see me.

I am standing tall, dark, and proud.

I have the power of a warrior.

Yeah, I said it out loud.

I am mighty in my own right.

Uniquely built and so heavenly precise.

See when I smile my cheekbones will rise oh so high, like the mighty clouds in the sky.

When I laugh you will hear a roar of thunder for I am glad that I did not take that trip down under.

For when I walk now my footsteps will be as soft as a gentle breeze.

I am upward bound pray someday that you will arrive here to see me.

I am just fine up here so please do not fret my dear.

I know that some are filled with sorrow and some are filled with pain.

However sweetheart you're not looking at what I've gained.

I've gained eternal life and a room in heaven with my heavenly father.

I've gained rights that I never knew that I'd have.

I am so proud to have been all that I could be.

So don't shed no tears of sorrow for me.

Leap and rejoice for my battle has been won and now I am free.

Upward Bound a poem that is truly one that is patterned after my own heart because my mom asked me to write this after the death of my grandmother.

I was hesitant at first because I was grieving and I felt that I lacked what I needed to concentrate on my writing.

Well it was the morning that I was to leave for Wisconsin and I had nothing on paper and I was becoming even more discouraged so I began to pray.

It was at that moment that God gave me Upward Bound. The words were coming so fast I couldn't even read them as I was writing.

After I had completed the poem I read it to myself and I wept because I knew that those words were given to me by God.

It proves that no one has the right to sit in judgement of someone else especially when they aren't aware of that person's pain.

« CHAPTER 53 »

Wait on Me!

As I woke up this morning I pray then say,

"Please God wait on me!"

As I prepare for my trialful day I pray then say,

"Please God wait on me!"

As I sit in awe of everything around me I pray then say,

"Please God wait on me!"

As I think of my life and all that I've done I pray then say,

"Please God wait on me!"

Then I look around and see flowers, trees, stars, the waters in the rivers flowing so free.

I then knew that God was standing right next to me saying,

"Please my child pray, and then, wait on me!"

Wait On Me! Was another one of those ah-ha moments in my life when I stopped to listen to God. I was going through so much and again overwhelmed by life.

I was asking God to be my help and was also questioning why it appeared that I was always being left behind.

It was then that God let me see that it was not him that was leaving me but rather I was the one leaving him.

That was a moment in my life that left me stunned and even amazed because throughout all of my trials and tribulations I did not stop to think that I was running away from God and not to him.

I would get angry and even blame God for allowing bad things to happen to me.

However, at that moment I realized that I allowed those bad things to happen to me because of my disobedience to God. It is often painful to accept responsibility for the negative events in our lives.

« CHAPTER 54 »

Welcome

Welcome one, welcome all.

I welcome those of which who may be mighty and tall or magnificent and called.

To those of which that are talented in their own way.

Unique and sweet no matter the time or day.

I bring you a welcome per-say.

I bid you a welcome on this glorious day for which we will praise the Lord and Savior in every way.

Our doors are always open to you for worship, prayer, and a song or two, that's just to name a few.

A handshake to greet a friend.

A tender hug with kind intent.

A gracious smile worth more than money spent.

Well really there's no other way to say that we welcome you with open arms on this very auspicious day.

So I give you this priceless gift.

A heartfelt welcome from me and it's given with respect and spiritual consent.

Welcome came about when yet again I was asked to write a welcome for the church program. I again did not think that I had what was required to do so.

To be even more honest I did not think that I even knew how to welcome anyone anywhere because of who I thought that I was.

So I got out a few books to see if I could find something to go by. Well needless to say that was a mistake because nothing in those books fit me nor the occasion so I began to pray.

Then I thought about how I had grown up to respect others no matter what we had or didn't have I still knew how to treat people. I also knew how I wanted to be treated and how I wanted someone to welcome me whether it was in church or someone's home.

« CHAPTER 55 »

What It's Like to Be Me?

What is it like to be happy?
What is it like to be free?
What is it like for the moment just to be me?
It's like a lawn full of grass getting mowed.
A tree in the fall right before it snows.
A pool covered with plastic as the summer ends.
A life full of pain and no friends.
What is it like for the moment just to be me?
It's like living a life with no hope, faith, or dreams.
Alone, alone, alone as hard as it is to be.
My heart aches for companionship, not sympathy.
What is it like for the moment to be me?
It's like blue skies turned gray on a cloudy day.
A bird chirping as the day comes to an end.
A life taken by your closest friend.

What is it like for the moment just to be me?
It's like looking for love in a world filled with hate.
A rose wilting away in a vase.
A closet full of clutter and very little space.

What it's Like to Be Me is a poem that I decide to write using metaphors to show how life can sometimes make me feel.

It is so very difficult sometimes when you feel that the whole world is upon your shoulders. But I did not want to just say that, I wanted to acknowledge the way that I was feeling in association to a few other events in life.

I often wondered if anyone else thought of some of the events in their lives as being like that of a natural disaster.

When times are hard I feel like I am in a thunderstorm and one wrong shift of the wind would leave me spiraling out of control.

However, when those good times come it's like one of those summer days when the weather is mild and there's not a dark cloud in the sky or when the grass, trees, and flowers are all green and in full bloom. When there is no sort of wrong and nothing is on my schedule to be doomed.

« CHAPTER 56 »

When You Came into My World

With open arms I accept thee into my world full of splendor and swirls.

You will always be a part of me for with thee I will forever be.

For a moment in time I only dreamed of what I thought thee, would be.

Tears of joy that flood my face as visions of you grace my individual mind and space.

Captured by your open and outspoken heart.

Ravished by the charm you so gallantly spread across as we seem to be miles apart.

Touched by the unseen and unforsaken spark that I felt across the room.

As the day before my life was that of never ending doom.

Given up on my dreams until I was touched by your vision, poise, and that determined face.

Come into my world and stay forever for however long that will be as it is undetermined by neither of us, only God has that vision to see and that authority to say.

For I will try and pray for that is the only way.

When You Came into My World was written with anticipation in mind. A title that I guess could lead your imagination to go off into several different areas because people enter your life for several different reasons.

We as human beings would want those meetings to be remarkably for the best and those individuals to put our best interest at heart.

However, often we are searching for the wrong things when we began a new relationship.

Too much emphasis is put on the other person's ability to make you happy when that is truly not where happiness lies.

You are the only one responsible for your happiness and if you give up that ability to allow yourself to be happy then whatever transpires is your own fault.

Love yourself enough to know that your fate is in God's hands and that by relying on him you will get to where you need to be.

« CHAPTER 57 »

Where I'd Be?

I often wonder where I'd be if I had telepathy.

Would I be short on mistakes and have many fulfilled dreams or would I be telling fortunes for whatever it may seem?

Would I be a superstar just gliding down the boulevard by far or would I be a glamour Queen seeking out more successful things.

I often wonder where I'd be if I had been born someone other than me.

Would I be from a perfect home in a perfect place?

Within a perfect time with perfect space.

Would I ever be a step above the rest?

The answer to that is no, when you're from a world filled with a lifetime of loneliness.

I often wondered where I'd be if I had held on to at least one of my dreams.

Would I have succeeded at being the best or would I have ended it in mere utter-ness?

Who knows where I'd be had I tried harder at being me.

Ah-ha, there it is, the key.

Stop trying so hard to be someone other than me.

Stand up, step out, look around and see there's no one, absolutely no one better at being me.

Comparisons, failed wages are sometimes all I can see but life goes on as I awaken to see that yet again I am still left here to just be me.

Where I'd Be, a poem about total acceptance of oneself and having the ability to gasp the very real concept that it is phenomenal being who God created you to be.

No one on this planet can be you better than you can. So bask it that knowledge and full joy being you.

« CHAPTER 58 »

Who Holds the Key

Who holds the key to the chains that bind me?

Bound by the thoughts that threaten to cripple all that God has ordained me to be.

Who, I say, who, holds the key to the chains that bind me?

Created free, and then captured by defeat, willing the freedom to come after me.

Who holds the key to the chains that bind me?

Stretching forth my hand while praying for the man that bound and gagged me.

He's telling me sweet lies while singing cryptic lullabies.

Who, I say, who, holds the key that binds me?

Eyes so rare, skin so soft, flair still there.

But there's no depth to the eyes, shine to the skin, nor compassion to the flair.

I look around and wonder how did I get there.

There in a place filled with shamed, betrayal, and disgrace, while plastic smiles are on everyone's face.

Who holds the key to the chains that bind me?

Hand to my heart, the other to my head wondering why I feel so empty, lost, and dead.

Searching for the me I use to be.

Wondering why I let these chains bind me?

Broken from memories that flood my mind.

Trying to stop the dam from breaking before I run out of time.

Mauled, maimed, torn into tiny pieces wondering if I can mend what use to me, completeness.

Who, I say, who, holds the key to the chains that bind me?

Rocking myself the way a loving mother soothes her crying baby.

Patting my own back and cheering myself on, looking for an outlet to escape from this raging storm.

The clouds have thickened, the sun has gone, the darkness nears me as I try to hold on.

Who holds the key to the chains that bind me?

This storm is stronger than I could have ever imagined and I feel saddened when I look at the damage she has left behind.

Catastrophe has caught up and bound me, crippling my feet, blocking my path, knocking me straight on my ass.

Who, I say, who, holds the key that binds me?

Who Holds the Key? A title that came to me as I was working on another project and frustrated by the lack of progress and wondering when the writer's block would lift itself off of me.

Then it lifted and I wasn't prepared. I was having a hard time keeping up because the words were coming so fast.

When I finished I was very pleased because the piece was nice and just what I needed to get me past that stumbling block.

« CHAPTER 59 »

Why Must I?

How do I categorize myself?

Well let me count the ways.

I often find myself having very unsightly days.

Joined at the hips by problems that have me dismayed.

Ready to walk away from all that surrounds me and those that have me in a daze.

I often ask myself why did I start this all?

Was it just to fail at the task of this unworthy cause.

I fail at everything that I do, even being born wasn't my cue.

As I often look around myself and see everyone else all happy and laughing at me.

Because I am a personal joke always being lied too, always being broken, always put last, always so sad.

Even when I'm laughing outside, I'm also crying inside.

Never a special song, never a special dance, never a special cause to give me a sweet glance.

Why must I settle?

Why must I suffer too?

Why am I on earth?

Is it to be a last place cue?

I am tired of dirty diapers, sick of sleep in my eyes.

Fed up with those never ending lies.

Why must I suffer?

When will it end?

Why can't I be the one to get the good surprise, instead of an unfaithful friend.

I pray for my blessings and some help from God please!

To get me through my never ending dreams.

Of always being swamped, of always being unappreciated, and never being put at ease.

I ask you now, someone help me please!

Why Must I? is another title written during a painful transition. It took a lot for me to get to the point where I would ask God to be my help because I felt unworthy.

I have struggled with learning to let go of my pride for as long as I could remember.

So my advice to you would be to please learn early that no matter what you are feeling God feels your pain too and therefore he has the ability to comfort you when you are feeling comfortless.

« CHAPTER 60 »

Worm

Sliding through this atmosphere.

Slithering and wondering if you're near.

Hoping and praying that you don't step on me.

On the other hand, going to heaven does sound rather unique.

My movements become rather instinctive relating to those other creatures bigger than me.

How about that I'm a worm sliding through the earth.

Wow, I'm free to be me.

Worm was a title given to me by my family. They challenged me to write a poem about a worm in one minute.

We were all gathered together after a family member's funeral just laughing and talking when I began to recited some of my previous work with them when the challenge was throw at me. A test as you will, to see just how good I was.

Well, that's what I came up with. It was a very difficult thing to do with a room full of people talking and purposely distracting me and not to mention the time of one minute that I was given. The pressure was on.

« CHAPTER 61 »

Your Touch

With the rub of my thigh, with the nibble of my breast, with the kiss of my lips, it all equals your sweet and gentle caress.

As the sweat glides down your brow.

I often wonder how?

How a man could make love to me like this.

With such passion and tenderness.

As I lay down on your rugged and sexy body.

I gaze into the windows of your soul.

As I listen to the gentle mourning you make, I began to think, oh for goodness sake.

A man so strong, dark, and proud.

A man so heavenly made and I often wonder how?

As I study your physique, it is so wonderfully unique and made just for me.

A luxurious African Queen.

Your Touch was written in accordance with the feeling that we receive when we are touched by someone that we love.

It is truly amazing what the human touch can do for a person. We all desire to be touched whether it be by holding someone's hand, receiving a hug, a kiss on the cheek, or in the mist of passion.

Just to know that someone cares enough to show compassion to you in the form of a loving touch.

We are created to be loving and affectionate beings. It is purely natural to crave for companionship. We all want to be acknowledged and desired.

The key to our survival is love and in order to receive love you must give it.

God's intention is for us to love one another.

APPENDIX

I am thankful for the journey that this life has taken me on. My life and all that I hope to be is because of who I am in the sight of El Shaddai. The emptiness that I have felt my entire life in this human body has only been filled by the Holy Spirit. I embrace and accept who I am in the body of The Almighty. As painful as this life has been for me, I will not give up, let up, nor hold up, for this is my destiny. I am predestined to be who I am and there is no changing that.

I am walking in my purpose. I am not becoming who I thought I needed to be. I am however finally functioning and operating as who I have always been. I am so thankful to God for pushing me to accept who I am and for teaching me how to allow that which needs to be, to be. I am not longer afraid of my spiritual gifts. I am finally at a place in my life where I am actually embracing my gifts and welcoming them. I now look forward to what my spirit is going to show me next and I no longer have the longing to be that which I know that I already am.

I am encouraged when I see the woman I am. I can even smile at the thought of all I have had to endure in order to allow her to burst forward and take the reins. I am excited to know that I am no longer pretending to be someone that I am not. I am living in my reality and I am proud of that fact. See, it is that spiritual reality that has me smiling at myself because that gives me hope that all that I have endured was

not in vain. It was because I was continuously denying who YHWH knew that I was and needed me to be. All of the suffering was due to this fact. I want all YHWH wants for me and I want my spirit to continue to lead me in order for my flesh to operate in the fullness thereof. The spirit is always before the flesh. It is unfortunate that this society thinks that the body rules, it is this misconception that gets us into trouble in the spirit realm and in the natural. The denial of the spirit always leads us astray.

I am very aware that the body has needs and I am aware that the spirit has needs. I am also aware that when the spiritual needs are met first then the needs of the body will surely follow. The spirit will make sure that the body has what it needs. We must first allow the spirit to do what is required. Always know that we are first SPIRITUAL and then NATURAL. SELAH.

NOTES

Victoria Amidou is also the author of "EL SHADDAI" which is now available in print and EBook.

Victoria Amidou has a Spoken Word album titled "FOR TRUE" which is now available.

AUTHOR LINKS

www.victoriaamidou.com
www.facebook.com/victoriaamidou
www.twitter.com/victoriaamidou
www.instagram.com/victoriaamidou
www.youtube.com/victoriaamidou
www.periscope.com/victoriaamidou

OVERVIEW

Poetically Me is my collection of poems. I wrote them over a span of many years at different stages of my life as I navigated my way through the twists and turns in my battle with myself.

From heartfelt pain, to a heart filled with joy. I have triumphantly emerged from the depths of despair as this journey has been my spiritual awakening.

This journey has led me to have a better relationship with myself and most importantly with God.

In all things I have finally begun to be at peace with the way that I am and with the things that have happen to me. Every event was used by God to draw me nearer to him and for that I am eternally thankful.